Michael Binnie

Grieg's Piano Concerto in Calcutta

dorcas imprints

First Edition: Grieg's Piano Concerto in Calcutta
First published in Great Britain in 2014 by:
dorcas imprints
Cookworthy Moor
Halwill
Beaworthy
Devon
EX21 5UU

www.indigodreams.co.uk

dorcas imprints is an imprint of Indigo Dreams Publishing Ltd

Michael Binnie has asserted his right under the Copyright, Designs
and Patents Act 1988 to be identified as the author of this work.
© Michael Binnie 2014

ISBN 978-1-909357-49-5

British Library Cataloguing in Publication Data. A CIP record for
this book can be obtained from the British Library.

Designed and typeset in Palatino Linotype by Indigo Dreams.
Cover design by Alex Binnie web: alexbinnie.com
Printed and bound in Great Britain by Imprint Academic, Exeter.

Papers used by Indigo Dreams are recyclable products made from
wood grown in sustainable forests following the guidance of the
Forest Stewardship Council.

For my wife, children and grandchildren;
for my sister; and for my friends.

PREFACE

The poems in this book are a selection of those I have written between 1965 and 2011. I am grateful to fellow poets in the Guildford society of Wey Poets with whom I shared many of the poems and who did much to encourage and help me shape them into their present form.

None of these poems would have appeared in print without the support of my wife, Carol, and the skill and patience of my granddaughter, Reika Binnie, who assembled them into the order that they appear here.

ACKNOWLEDGEMENTS

Two of these poems appeared in *Weyfarers:* one in *Outposts* and another in the journal of The Climbers' Club. *Summer Term* was a prize winner in the Wells Festival of Literature 2011.

CONTENTS

SAFETY PRECAUTIONS 9

CLINIC 10

HAPPINESS NEAR BRIGHTON 11

IN PATIALA 12

NIGHT NOISES 14

ANGELS 15

PUNJAB 16

LISTENING TO MOZART WITH GUY 17

FIRST IMPRESSIONS 18

TOWARDS LONDON 19

YESTERDAY AT LUNCHTIME 20

JULIUS AND ETHEL ROSENBERG ENQUIRE ABOUT
THEIR MOVE INTO TEMPORARY ACCOMMODATION 21

NEAR COLDSTREAM 23

DID YOU KNOW 24

SUMMER TERM 25

WATER 26

SHOSTAKOVICH STRING QUARTET 27

WATER WHEEL 28

RAAG 29

HAPPINESS IN THE HINDU KUSH 30

OCTOBER 31

NEAR EDINBURGH 1945-50 32

SONATA 33

SAILING TO WINDWARD 34

LEAVING INSTRUCTIONS 35

GRIEG'S PIANO CONCERTO IN CALCUTTA 36

AT WATERLOO 37

FINLAND 38

AFTER SREBRENICA 39

JESS 40

CHRISTMAS EVE, CHICAGO 41

BOSIGRAN 42

FRANCE, 2007 43

APRÉS LE DEUXIÈME BIVOUAC 45

IN CHITRAL 46

DREAM BIRDS 47

Grieg's Piano
Concerto in Calcutta

SAFETY PRECAUTIONS

"Never
drink unboiled water
and if an Indian comes at you
with a knife do not
under any circumstances
(under any circumstances
underlined)
attempt to grapple with him.
A kick in the stomach will suffice."
So ended my father's letter of advice.

Next day I Boeinged
to Delhi where Mr. Sharma's
gentle brother rescued me
from the buzzing airport,
took me to his hot-house
of a house,
sat me in a chair
and poured a lime and water drink
from an earthenware pot.
"Please take," he said, "this is
good for the stomach."

Beyond the spinning fan
my father's face revolved with
"thirty years experience of the country"
and mouthed a thousand warnings through
the blurring whirr...the whirring blur, yet
"Is it boiled?" stuck in my throat
as Mr. Sharma's brother advanced
to within grappling distance.

CLINIC

My orthoptist, Mrs. Penrose
is beautiful and wears black.
Her smile is a poker hand
held tight to the chest. Today
she is dressed in blue and I want to say,
"You look lovely," but am restrained
by the demands of propriety.
We sit opposite each other, my face
a foot from her face, my eyes
stitched to the pencil she holds
before me. Momentarily my eyes
slip into her eyes. She speaks sharply,
"No, the pencil please." I stand
by the door waiting to leave, wanting
to say something. Anything. Then
together we hear a shout of childish
laughter outside in the corridor.
In a burst of impulse I cast inhibition
aside. "Do you have children?"
And slowly she reveals her ace,
a smile like a summer's evening,
the tide rising on a beach towards
picnics, sandcastles, cricket games
and excited dogs. My orthoptist.
Mrs Penrose.

HAPPINESS NEAR BRIGHTON

Everyone who came to Alex's fiftieth
loved him. You could tell. All afternoon
there was a fine rain but still they came to the beach.
A number by bus plus a few who walked.
And mostly the old crowd.
Mark the clarinet player and Hughey
who lived in a squat. Several tattooists.
Christine, who espoused nudism and threw pots,
together with her sister Jen, who painted.
And Mim who was a dancer and performance artiste.
Also a man who made things in leather
for the kinky trade, together with his tattooed wife.
That sort of crowd. Yoga enthusiasts.
Herbal tea drinkers. Not an investment banker
or ship broker amongst them. Plus Alex's
Amber and Angus who played on the rocks
with some other kids. After the picnic
Jen got out a violin and played Happy Birthday
after which we all sang, very softly,
For He's a Jolly Good Fellow.
Then we all changed into swim suits, save Christine,
and followed Alex in his leggings of Maori coils,
with the Angel Gabriel glistening on his back,
into the sea at Rottingdean, in the rain, last summer.

IN PATIALA

When Dogra came to tea
we swept the dust under the carpet
and spruced up. His family
were Rajputs, fighters.
Bang on the dot at four o'clock,
he stood at the door, shirt and pants
pressed, moustache
neat and trim as a military line.
He talked in a staccato bark
and precisely at six swung away
in quick time. He liked
a good laugh, a bottle of beer,
plenty of exercise
and our children. In the mind's eye
he sits astride a black charger
sweeping the countryside
like some ancient warrior king.
He managed a shop selling spares
for tractors and tube wells.

Om Prakash arrived
at any old time invariably
wearing the same dishevelled
shirt and stayed for hours.
He loved music and the great poets.
Deep into the night we sat in the garden
and listened to records of flute
and sitar. Occasionally
he spoke quietly.
"This is early morning music.
It should be played softly
and heard across water."
Om Prakash loved God
and ate no meat

for he was a Brahmin.
When he came he brought gifts,
a few bread fruits or wild honey
for he was a teacher and not a rich man.

NIGHT NOISES

Long into the night
loud-speakered songs from the city
drone across a mile of military lines
and into the peeling rooms of this gaunt house.
The punkah flaps and wrestles with the air.
We lie in bad staring into the dark.

Ninety years ago a maharajah built this house
for his caste off wives. One by one
when their time was up at the palace
down the road he sent them packing here.
There were thirty seven in all.
Each night they stir to life.
We hear delicate footfalls, murmurs, even
moans as these faded wives recall
distant moments of ecstasy.
The screeching love songs from the city
mingle with these lost voices.
Slowly the air tucks itself round us like a blanket
and we are smothered to sleep.

At dawn the noises are a half-forgotten dream.
It is cool now, the shadows are dispelled.
The phantom women have slunk into corners and cupboards,
nursing the secrets of their hearts.

ANGELS

As a little boy I had this worry about Heaven.
When we died and became angels
what happened to our legs
when we flew? Did they stick out behind us
like a stork's or curl up under our bodies
like a sparrow's?
My parents pondered this with me one night
while dressing up to go out,
my father in shirt sleeves tying his black tie
with characteristic neatness,
my mother at her dressing table
lining her eyes.
I caught their indulgent smiles in the mirror.
They favoured the stork option.
And now Dad's gone.

Sometimes I think of him up there,
legs extended, flapping ponderously about
or soaring in great circles with all the other storks,
waiting for us to join him.

PUNJAB

The wind pulls and tears at your face like a blunt razor.

The sun bores into your marrow like an infra-red lamp.

The wells are like misers.

The earth is like a dried up walnut.

The sky is like a painting with no colour at all.

The mynahs gasp in a mango tree
like a line of patients at the doctor's saying "Aah."

The Coppersmith mocks with his call like a dripping tap.

The Brain Fever Bird has the laugh of a man
with a twisted sense of humour.

This crazy month! Something got jammed in the works
when God created May.

LISTENING TO MOZART WITH GUY

Entering a room and hearing a snatch of the Clarinet Concerto
on Classic FM. The slow movement.
I think of Guy.

A man with whom I had gone to school.
Who would one day become my best man.
The afternoons spent in his digs our first term at Keble.
Sharing the unfamiliar. Struggling to make our mark.
Listening to the Horn Concertos.
Stuff I can't listen to any more but our signature
all that term. Guy lolling, cigarette
dangling from his stained fingers.
And, boy, did he make his mark.
A man who smoked Rothmans and bought his clothes
in St. James'. Who did insouciance in spades.
A man who collected people, whom people
wanted to know. Whose approbation I craved.
But never acquired. Whose life once kissed mine
before it went for broke, the City, the yacht,
the vortex. Down the tubes.
With whom I used to listen to the Horn Concertos
in Blackhall Road. Who would one day
become my best man. But never his best friend.
Now fading into something by Bach.

FIRST IMPRESSIONS

This is the day
I am to be made a man.
Today I am ordered to report
to the Regimental Headquarters.

The border town is full of young men
who assume nonchalance, pretend
they have plenty to do. All morning
we roam the streets, avoiding each other,
looking at our watches and ourselves in shop windows
checking the shortness of our hair.

Yesterday Father sent me to the barbers.
"Best to make a good impression.
I should wear your double breasted blazer
and the Old School tie."
When I reach the barracks I'm directed
to my sleeping quarters and sit
on the bare springs of my bed
in a vacant room. A corporal comes in
who is large and brisk who says
"Bedding will be drawn at eighteen hundred hours."
Later I am joined by Billy who was a miner
and a Ted, then Jock and Adam
who were both in the building trade.
When one of them asks,
"What did you do?" I tell them,
"I was at school."

Weeks later, one Saturday night at closing time,
we will stand together on the pavement
and swear life long loyalty to each other.
But now we are four strangers
in this bleak room with empty shelves
and naked beds and I am wondering
whether I am making a good impression.

TOWARDS LONDON

Yesterday morning I saw Gunter Grass standing
on the platform at Wimbledon Station. Yes!
Anyway it looked like him. That same hang-dog face
and heavy moustache, peering over his glasses
like he does in the photos. Wearing a black
leather coat down to his knees and a small
rucksack. And looking bewildered
before disappearing behind an incoming train.
Next my compartment filled up
with fourteen year old kids. Polite, well behaved
children with pale, flat faces. And talking Russian!
First that German fellow at Wimbledon and now
the air resonant with Slavonic vowels. "Ye-es,"
they said when I asked them, "We are Russians.
We come from Russia." Their teacher and I
exchanged smiles. In my day Russian women
were Soviet discuss throwers.
This one had the body of a go-go dancer.
When she pointed to Big Ben and the Parliament buildings
the children responded with casual indifference
and soon looked away or into their smart phones.
So as we crept into Waterloo I alone
was left clinging to the words of this girl from the steppes
with the golden hair and bedroom eyes
as she lectured passionately about democracy,
votes for women and all that incomprehensibly.

YESTERDAY AT LUNCHTIME

Yesterday at lunchtime you leaned across to me and said,
"Let's not die yet."
We'd been talking of death that morning.
Had been, on and of, for days. I knew
that I had never loved you so much as I did then.
I said, "If only I had a portrait of you painted in oils."
You laughed. "Of me forty years ago?"
"No, now."

It's true, your teeth no longer have that startling gap,
middle of the top row, with which I fell in love.
A Khyber Pass, a South Col of a gap. Gone now
after a thousand pounds worth of reconstruction.
And your feet, first loved – still loved – that summer
on Elba. In your new sandals, legs crossed, for the painting?
Or bare, perhaps, your right tucked under your thigh,
your left hanging over the floor, toenails cherry red.
And those hands, which search me out each night
before sleep. Folded in your lap in the portrait?
No…no. I want you reaching out for the slice of mango
I've just peeled, your fingers absorbed into mine,
before dissolving up to your mouth. Followed by your eyes
crinkling into that mascara wrecking smile
at me across the lunchtime table.

JULIUS AND ETHEL ROSENBERG ENQUIRE ABOUT THEIR MOVE INTO TEMPORARY ACCOMMODATION

In June 1953 the Rosenbergs were electrocuted in Sing Sing prison New York for betraying nuclear secrets to Soviet Russia. It was widely believed that Ethel had been wrongly convicted. The night before their death they sat in their cell with their two little boys telling stories and playing cards.

Sing Sing? Indeed
it is a pretty name.
What can I say?
The property comprises
several acres of secluded
grounds (high security
is rigorously maintained round
the clock by fully trained
professionals) with scenic
vistas overlooking the Hudson
(outstanding colours
in the Fall) though we regret
that you are unlikely to be
given a room with a view.
Your length of stay
will be determined by
bureaucratic decisions
beyond our control.
You will be provided
with fully furnished
twin bed accommodation
with en-suite facilities.
You may find the food
on the monotonous side
but anyway you will soon be
moving on. Finally
I might mention that
there will be no charge
for water, gas or electricity

and should there be
a failure of the latter our
in-house generators will
provide enough surges of
power to satisfy every
foreseeable requirement.

NEAR COLDSTREAM

All my life I've thought about that day.
Anyway for fifty one years
which is as much as some people ever live.
So I count myself lucky.
How we walked through fields of ripening corn
and meadows with cattle grazing
till we reached the river. Each of us just twenty.
Soldiers escaped from the barracks for the afternoon.
Demob happy. In ten minutes
arriving at a curve on the Tweed. The river
that separates one country from another.
Throughout my life I've marvelled at that day.
Told my wife about it.
Told her how we threw off clothes,
number, name and rank that July afternoon
and plunged into the stream. How we swam
to England then floated into the Congo,
currents like bathwater coiling round our bodies
before freezing into the Yukon. For an hour
we played in the river by woods and grassy banks.
Diving amongst the salmon. Within weeks
Cpl. Mather was back, harvesting the corn,
for those were his father's fields and cattle.

I think of him now, carroty hair long gone,
family picnic by the water's edge,
watching his grandchildren paddling at his feet,
and remembering, perhaps, the day that he too
stood on the bank, naked as these kids,
with that officer fellow from the regiment,
and wondering if life had dealt him
a half decent hand. If somewhere, some time,
there had been other summer afternoons.
Other rivers.

DID YOU KNOW

She said
that you smell
of your house.
Your coat too.
Of the damp,
the fire. Also
the dogs.
And your garden.
The grass,
the woods,
the fields
and distant valleys.
The far ranges.
That old coat.
Which I've known
for fifteen years.
All my life.
And that waistcoat
which I told you
once I wanted
when you die.
To keep your
smell. Of your
house, the smoke,
the damp walks.
Of you.
Your smell.
You.

SUMMER TERM

Last summer. Like none other since 1976
when the earth opened out into cracks
and houses threatened to collapse.
The summer I took the girls swimming
at Winkworth. Changed in the field
below the arboretum and jumped in, screaming.
Then swam round the lake in a flotilla.
One time a man called down to us,
"You look like Konrad Lorenz with his cygnets."
My class of eight. Shouting to each other,
faces streaming. That skinny Beccy, beaten up
by her father whom she never stopped loving
and Louella picked up by the police
for soliciting outside the train station.
Mandy, thrown out from one foster home after another.
"Binnie, why can't I go and live with my mum?"
Those girls. Who hated boarding and whose bile
I suffered daily. Maths, History. The usual stuff
that passes for education. Also occasionally
poetry. Kipling and that one of Auden's,
Oh what is that sound, about the soldiers
smashing into a house to conscript their man.
Acted it out in class. Six goose stepping girls
marching closer and closer, Beccy
pleading with her husband not to leave her,
the door thrown down and her terrible scream
echoing to every corner of Tillingbourne House.
Two years hard at the chalk face. Squeezed
through the mangle. Sharing my life with those kids.
Decimal points, the Black Death. Swimming.

WATER

This man I know has to live beside water.
And not any water. A river. For months,
even years, he scoured the country
searching for his dream. Finally struck gold.
Found somewhere he could plant a garden.
Bring his young wife. Raise a family.
Now every morning he looks across the islands
and sand banks of the Severn near Purton.
Each morning he breathes the salt air
and watches the movement of the tides
with the eye of an expert.
A man who can navigate this river.
Has a feel for its water.
Who once crossed the Oxus on the back of a horse
then rode it alone through Afghanistan.
A man who knows about horses and rivers.
Who throws open his house to his friends,
takes them onto his lawn to admire
what he cannot live without and tells them,
"*Me casa es tu casa.*" Then tips back his head
and laughs. That kind of a man.

SHOSTAKOVICH STRING QUARTET

I hear violins whispering to the trees.

From inside a darkened room in May
Violins are whispering to trees
Dancing outside. And the voice in the music says
Free me! Free me!

But the leaves can't hear. The people
Won't hear, daren't hear. The people
Are too frightened or too happy with a moment's
Snatched happiness to hear the voice
Like an ash pit pressed to the bars again cry
Free me! Free me!

It is too terrible and dark.
There is thunder of crashed chords,
Thunder and gallop of Cossack squadrons
The air taut with plucked strings,
The bow held high like a sabre
And the scream from the violins is
No! No! No! No! No!

WATER WHEEL

They have left the youngest of the family
at the water wheel.
He squats in the shade of a scrubby tree
all day, playing his little boy games
of sticks and stones in the dry earth,
or like a stork stands on one leg
supported by his staff, while his camel
blindfolded, like a man at a firing squad,
shambles his body round pouring water
onto the shit-encrusted plain.
There is no future at this well. Only
the historic present. The ears of wheat
will barely reach my knees.
The little boy has his dreams.

RAAG

The sitar
rolls her eyes
strikes bold poses
with fingers
and soft thighs
while the tabla gulps
discreetly in the
background.

HAPPINESS IN THE HINDU KUSH

Now the valley has widened into a plain
garnished with hedge rows of wild
roses and poplars. Herd boys
gallop about playing bare back polo.
Their sisters sit in the sunshine
combing each others hair. Everywhere
is the rhapsody of skylarks. When people ask,
"Where are you going?" I say, "to Lashkergaaz."
I fall in with a young man on a pony,
the colour of lightly-done toast, who asks,
"Are you a doctor?" I say, "No,"
but give him some tablets for his hurt leg.
He leans down to shake my hand
then kisses the back of his own
before cantering off into a wood, twisting
and turning through the trees like a Cossack
in a scene from Doctor Zhivago.

OCTOBER

Walking in the wood this Sunday morning,
the dogs mincing over spiny chestnut cases,
their spilt nuts glistening like the flanks
of groomed hunters. Remembering
how yesterday we had said to each other,
"How lucky we are." And how often we say it.
Let's not die yet. That's another poem I wrote.
Beyond the wood children are playing
in the riding ring at the stables. I rejoice
in the screams of the little girls jumping
on and off their ponies, practising
for the gymkhana. The dogs crouch,
watching me, anxious to move off
but I stand my ground and listen.
You cannot be happier than those girls.
Or children pouring into the playground
at break, the shrill roar of their happiness.
The oratorio of childhood. Or a young woman
walking home, holding her little boy's hand,
laughing, telling him about the treat
he'll be having for his tea. Can you beat that?

NEAR EDINBURGH 1945-50

Today I am thinking of obdurate, red-headed Sym,
who escaped on the last boat out of Singapore in '41.
Who knew no fear. Who spat upon authority. Who fought
an endless war of attrition with Mr. Mylne aged ten,
then eleven. Twelve. But bore his floggings with a smirk.
Whose shadow one crossed at one's peril.
Then at thirteen disappeared, slipped out of our lives.
So no longer the fraught glance over the shoulder,
the quick reflexes, the involuntary defensive move.

But now I think of Sym the five year old little boy,
clinging to his mother at each crash of the Japanese
guns, the whine of the Zero fighters. The scramble
to board the ship, leaving behind his father
to face the music (women and children first).
Good bye Daddy. *Sym, who knew no fear.*

Who became a farmer in New Zealand. I see him now,
a tall gaunt figure,
ranging over the hills of the South Island with his sheep
and cursing his dog.

SONATA

It was said that during the worst years of the Terrors
Dmitri Dmitriyevich Shostakovich
would pack a suitcase and sleep on the landing
outside his apartment so that when they came to get him
his family would remain undisturbed.

Akhmatova remembers how he invited her to visit him at Repino.
"We sat together for twenty minutes without speaking.
It was wonderful."

He has less than a year to live and can barely hold a pen.
Late in the night he rings Druzhinin, the viola player,
to discuss his final composition.
"This passage should sound divine...
here the walls are collapsing around you...
play it so that flies drop dead in mid-air
and the audience start leaving the hall from sheer boredom."

SAILING TO WINDWARD

There is no direct route
to the line. Progress is made
by a series of tacks and is measured
in inches. Every other boat
appears to be pointing higher than us.
There are no easy answers plus
there is the problem of lee way.

My father sits at the helm peering
through the spray into his dreams,
steering his course through life
while I crouch amidships,
aged ten, twenty, thirty, forty
watching him pitch and roll, going about
just at the wrong moment, somehow
missing the tide, allowing his opponents
to squeeze him into the shallows, steal his wind.

He speaks to me gently.
"As we round the mark ease on the sheets
a little." We round the mark
and heel into a new chapter.
Things are going to look up from now.

LEAVING INSTRUCTIONS

Never underestimate the importance
of a good haircut.
Reply to an invitation
in the manner by which you were
invited. Do not be tempted
to hurry into your back swing
(and keep your eye firmly
on the ball). Be warned
that not every one
who went to Public School
is a gentleman.
As a general rule it is
better to bow too low than
not to bow low enough.
Always remember to keep
a sharp lookout for a lee shore.
Also I should mention that
though lamb may be carved thick
it is imperative that beef
should be thinly sliced.
Finally let me say that
it is usually wiser
to keep your mouth shut,
and be thought a fool,
than to open it
and remove all possible doubt.

GRIEG'S PIANO CONCERTO IN CALCUTTA

Summer hols. Aged sixteen. Afternoons
on the verandah of my parents house
in Alipore Park Road. Listening to Grieg.
Waiting for my father to return from the office
to take me to Tollygunge for a few holes
before dark. Each morning at the Swimming Club
and every evening golf at Tolly. One Sunday
we drove into the green landscape beyond the city
to shoot snipe with a man called Mervyn
who told me to forget that idea about school
being the happiest days of your life. Any girls
at your school? No. Just wait
till you get to the Varsity. A holiday
of amusement and concealed, simmering frustration.
Each night, my sister and I, sitting on the verandah
with our parents, playing cards. Somewhere
outside a man calling, selling ice creams
from his bike, *"Mag-no-li-a"*. Then sometimes
my father would get up and put on the Grieg,
half a dozen 78s played in succession
then reversed towards the end of the slow movement.
Over our garden wall you could see the lights
on a temple roof and between the intervals of each record
hear the chime of bells and the chanting of an evening hymn.

AT WATERLOO

One of those chance encounters. "Zoya!" "Mike!"
"Fancy meeting you!" "I know, and you!"
"How *are* you?" "Very well. How's Carol?"
The usual banalities. A girl I knew twenty five years ago
whom I appointed to teach at my school.
Who wore her hair like a boy's and had a penchant
for corduroys slung over hips as slim as a boys.
A woman so beautiful I would stand smiling to myself
just watching her cross the playground.
But unaware of her beauty. Wore it
without guile. Like an innocent savage.
A woman from the Empty Quarter
or the Sierra Nevada de Santa Marta.
One summer we took all the kids to the seaside for the day.
Everybody changed into their swimwear.
Zoya stepped out of her clothes into a white bikini
sprayed with a splash of polka dots in black.
Just imagine it. I had to look away.
All morning we played in the waves or at rounders
then assembled in rows with our sandwiches.
I sat behind Zoya.
I remember gazing at a line of pale hairs
in the small of her back, caught in the sunlight.
Hairs we all possess but never notice.
Zoya's silken down glimmering in the sunshine
at Climping. Now refusing a cup of coffee.
Anxious to escape the old boy in the funny glasses.
Pleading a train to catch. Drifting out of his reach.
Still sheathed in that unconscious pulchritude.

FINLAND

A lake
like an hour glass
and round it
a forest of spruce
and pine.
Shafts of sunlight
filtering through low cloud.
In the lake
a woman swimming.
A man stands
by a red hut
with white corners
and window frames
watching the woman
who swims to the shore
and emerges
in a green swimsuit
and walks
towards the man
who is holding
a blue towel.

AFTER SREBRENICA

The man is tall and thin. Haggard.
Deep lines on his cheeks resemble a shark's gills.
Lines of exhaustion and hunger.
You can tell he's been through it. Suffering
written all over him. Two women
cling to his sides. The one in a white top
with a fine head of hair tied back
must be his wife. His daughter
is wearing a dress patterned with the heads
of cartoon dogs. The women have broken down.
Their man has escaped the death squads.
Somehow he has got through the mountains
unharmed. For days they've lived on the brink,
anxiety eating into their very bowels.
And now they can't take it anymore. They've had it
up to here. So they sob into his crumpled coat
while he stands, head bowed, arms limp,
unable to hold his wife and daughter,
hollowed eyes witness to acts
of which he is unable to speak.

JESS

Woke last night from a dream about my mother
for whom I had always been ready with my time,
even, occasionally, been kind.
Visited once a week. Took her on picnics
and talked of the old days. The gay times in Bombay.
But never about the deep stuff.
Never about death. The fear of death.
In her last days sat holding her hand.
But never for long enough. Got up to drive home
before I needed to go. To whom I had never said,
"I love you." Last night she appeared in my dream.
Stood beside me in the kitchen, tiny and frail.
Took her in my arms.
Crushed her to me for the first time.
In the morning when I told you, you said,
"Now she knows. You've put it right."
So I feel better. An expiation.
Yet all day I've carried a wretchedness.
Wanting to turn the clock back.
Wishing I had said, if only once, "I love you."

CHRISTMAS EVE, CHICAGO

Her father said, "Remember the violin
grandpa gave you on your thirteenth birthday?"
The girl nodded vaguely
and looked out at the snowstorm.
Drifts were beginning to pile up
on the steps of the Art Institute.
"An Arctic air stream is edging South
into the Mid West,"
was what the man had said on the T.V.
"You played it in the Tchaikovsky
Violin Concerto," his voice choked.
She looked back blank.
Those days were past. Rev. Moon
was her new Father now.

Besides them the restaurant was empty.
It was beginning to get dark.
Everyone else had taken the bus home
or the El. By the counter three waitresses
were laughing and teasing each other.
"Remember?" he pleaded. Outside
the wind tossed an empty cardboard box
down the street and out of sight.

BOSIGRAN

At nine the air is magic.
From the cliffs Commando Ridge
bristles like a dragon's back
while behind the sun singes
into a black, burnt treacle sea.
Pendeen light flickers its warning jabs
and stabs ships out twenty miles.
We turn and head inland,
past an engine house and old shafts,
scabs on deep Cornish wounds.
These holes are like crushed mouths
and speak of the agony of miners.
Past all these onto the moor
where the carns become kopjes, the emptiness
a sweep of Africa and up to the circle
of nine standing stones. The Nine Maidens.
"Why are they called that, sir?"
"Well once upon a time…" and suddenly
a story bites deep as six London kids
crouch round, spell bound in the failed light
by an old legend which unfolds
to a backdrop of a rising moon and wind
tilting the grass. And when after the long silence
Richard says, "Imagine coming to this place,
all on your own, no one knowing about it,
hundreds of years ago, wouldn't it be fantastic?"
I know there is magic in the air at ten.

FRANCE, 2007

Sunday afternoon. October. Walking with my wife
and Anna by the great bend in the Rhone
near St. Genix-sur-Guiers.
Anna who is tall and thin and brave. Also
fabulously beautiful. But anxious.
Lines of anxiety etched onto her beautiful face.
But now relaxed. And happy. The three of us happy
in the sunshine, sauntering, and talking
about families, and the people we knew.
And the old days. Ah…the old days.
Should we swim? We have brought our things.
Within moments we are splashing and gasping
and laughing (especially laughing) and feeling
clean and good. Afterwards we drive
across the river to Maison d'Izieu, below white cliffs.
A limestone house with blue shutters
and an inscription carved into a granite plaque.
Memorial des enfants Juifs exterminés le 6 Avril 1944.
The morning that forty-four children sheltered here
were seized by the Gestapo. Toys, untouched since that day,
lie scattered on the floors. Letters to parents
remain unposted. Days later the children and their carers
are welcomed at the gates of Hell. Within hours
Auschwitz guards are shovelling up their bones.

Maman, my dear Maman,
I know how much you've suffered on my account and on this happy
occasion of Mother's Day I send you from afar my best wishes from
the bottom of my little heart. So far from you, darling Maman. I've
done everything I could to make you happy. When you've sent
packages I've shared them with children who have no parents.
Maman, my dear Maman, I leave you with hugs and kisses.
Your son who adores you. Jacques.

The three of us stand in the evening sun
on the terrace of Maison d'Izieu
where once the children played. We say nothing.
Below is a field of cows. Further off
the Rhone valley and the distant Chartreuse.
Anna is worried about Mark so we get into the car
and drive home quickly to find him
sitting alone in a room beside his Zimmer,
the light fading, waiting for us.

APRÉS LE DEUXIÈME BIVOUAC

A mountaineering guide of the 1940s and 50s

When I grow up I want to be called
Rébuffat. Gaston Rébuffat
from Marseille. I will have a shock
of black hair and long legs and live in a chalet
near Chamonix. I will speak French
with a nasal twang and appear in *Paris*
Match wearing snazzy dark glasses
and white cable-knit stockings. In the evenings
I will meet Terray and Lachenal in a bar
and talk about Annapurna.
I will walk up to the huts with my clients
wearing one of my expensive-looking
and photogenic sweaters. We will breathe
the night air in the starlight and moon glow
then climb in the dawn towards the slash
of a distant sunrise. And when I grow up
I will weather a storm on the Badile
with Bernard Pierre who will photograph me
on a ledge, my face twisted into an
anguished grimace after the second bivouac.

IN CHITRAL

Each morning we wake up thinking of home.
Summers are flashes of golden oreoles
amongst the poplars. Orchards are heavy
with apricots, mulberries, grapes and walnuts.
People tell us, "Your house is called Doaba
which means between two rivers. You
will be happy there and free from scorpions."
Everywhere is the sound of running water
and children playing. Winter sunrise
and the mountains finger the sky, vivid with snow.
Every morning we wake up thinking of home.

DREAM BIRDS

Which birds?

This hoopoe
forking the garden like a man busy in his allotment.

These parakeets
clinging to the walls of the fort like rock-climbers.

These orioles
streaking through the trees like gold-tipped arrow heads.

These vultures
crash-landing into the dirt like B 52 s.

These mynahs
striding about my lawn like leggy, bespectacled school girls.

This Red Wattled Lapwing
leaping into the air and screaming *Did-he-do-it! Did-he-do-it!*

These drongos
swaying on the telegraph wires like tight-rope artistes.

These kites
circling over the city like silent, secret policemen.

These Rollers
twisting in the air like Olympic gymnasts.

This kingfisher
poised over the river like Death.

These paddy birds
standing patiently in the shallows waiting…waiting.

These birds.

dorcas imprints
24, Forest Houses
Cookworthy Moor
Halwill
Beaworthy
Devon
EX21 5UU
www.indigodreams.co.uk